Amazing Science Discoveries

CHEMISTRY

The story of atoms and elements

Dr. Bryson Gore

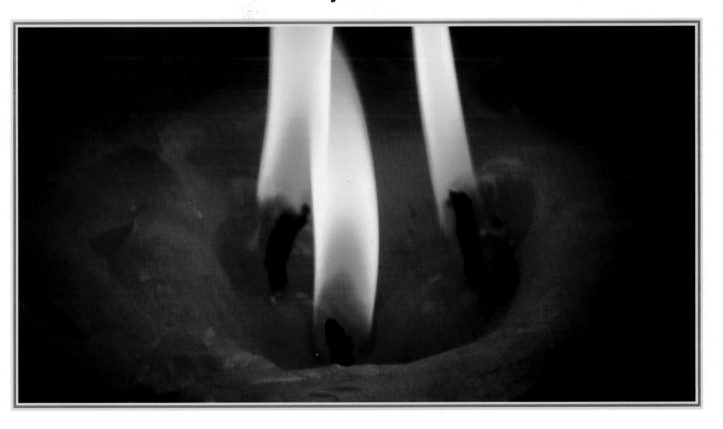

Aladdin / Watts

London • Sydney

CONTENTS

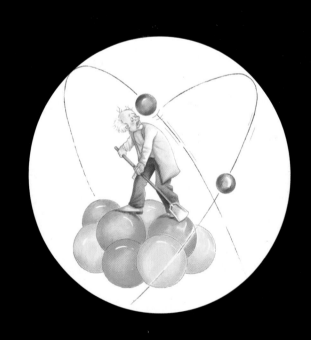

© Aladdin Books Ltd 2009

Designed and produced by Aladdin Books Ltd
PO Box 53987
London SW15 2SF

ISBN 978 0 7496 8648 2

First published in 2009
by Franklin Watts
338 Euston Road
London NW1 3BH

Franklin Watts Australia
Level 17/207 Kent Street
Sydney NSW 2000

Franklin Watts is a division of Hachette Children's
Books, an Hachette Livre UK company.
www.hachettelivre.co.uk

A CIP record for this book is available from the
British Library

Dewey Classification: 540

Printed in Malaysia

Editors: Katie Harker, Vivian Foster
Design: Flick, Book Design and Graphics
Illustrators: Q2A Creative
Picture research: Brian Hunter Smart

The author, Dr. Bryson Gore, is a freelance lecturer
and science demonstrator, working with the Royal
Institution and other science centres in the UK.

Introduction

Humans have puzzled over CHEMISTRY – the study of substances – for hundreds of thousands of years. What am I made from? Why does a certain food taste nice? By studying the material world and how it changes, we have been able to answer many of these questions.

In ancient times, people believed the world was made from four different elements – Earth, Air, Fire and Water. Around 1000 AD, alchemists started to carry out experiments.

Foolishly, they thought they could turn cheap metals into gold. Of course they failed.

About 300 years ago, modern chemistry took over. Chemists started to study the composition of rocks and minerals. They soon realised there were not just four elements, but dozens.

In the 20th century, biologists turned to chemists to help them understand 'proteins'. These are giant molecules that form the building blocks of all living things.

This book takes a look at twelve of the most amazing chemical discoveries that have taken place throughout history. Find out more about the famous chemists such as Mendeleev, Maillard and Avogadro. Learn how they used their skills to make sense of a complicated subject.

By reading the fact boxes you will start to understand topics such as elements, atoms and molecules. Learn about the power of energy, and the way different substances react to one another.

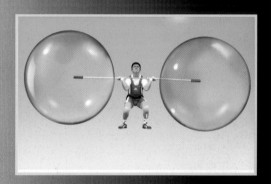

MERCURY IS THE ONLY LIQUID METAL

Everything in the world around us is made from elements, substances composed of minute particles called 'atoms'. One group of elements is called 'metals'. Metals are all very different. Some are extremely strong, some will melt if hot enough, while others are very soft. Mercury, however, is the only metal that is liquid at room temperature.

The science of . . .

There are about 110 different elements in the Universe.

Everything on Earth is built from around 80 of these elements. One of the most important tools in chemistry is the Periodic Table (see pages 7 and 30).

Roughly two-thirds of all elements are metallic. Metals on the left of the table are very reactive. Less reactive elements are in the centre, while non-metallic are on the right.

WOWZSAT!

When Mendeleev proposed the Periodic Table for chemical elements, he left a number of gaps. It was just as well – within six years three more were discovered.

How do we Know?

In 1869, a Russian chemist named Dimitri Mendeleev came up with an idea called the 'Periodic Table'.

Although he didn't know why elements were different from each other, he did know other details, such as their weight.

Mendeleev set about drawing a table. He put the lightest element – hydrogen (H) – in the top left corner, and the heaviest in the bottom right. He started a new line every time he came across an element that was similar to hydrogen. He soon noticed that a pattern was building up, and that the properties were repeating themselves periodically – hence the name 'Periodic Table'.

SCIENTISTS CAN TURN LEAD INTO GOLD

For hundreds of years, alchemists tried to turn lead into gold. They never succeeded. In the 1980s, however, physicists managed to change a few thousand atoms of lead into gold for the first time in history. The secret was the use of a nuclear reactor.

The science of . . .

In 1980, a physicist called Glenn Seaborg transformed thousands of atoms of lead into precious gold.

Seaborg discovered that by changing the atomic number in lead using a nuclear reactor, he could actually cause the lead itself to turn into precious gold.

Although the experiment was a success, the process was much too expensive for Glenn Seaborg to gain any wealth. But at least he proved it could be done.

How do we know?

About 100 years ago, scientists started to look inside atoms. They wanted to find what made one element different to another.

Using beams of radioactive particles called 'Alpha' particles, the scientists discovered that the mass of an atom is centred around its core (the nucleus).

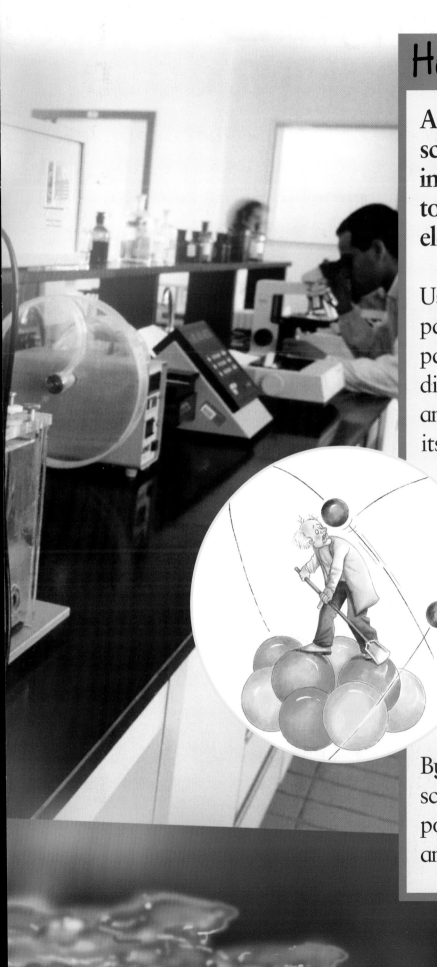

Inside the nucleus are three types of particle – protons, neutrons and electrons. Basically an atom is a delicate balance of both positive and negative forces.

By doing this type of research, scientists proved that it was possible to alter the nucleus of an atom by using radioactivity.

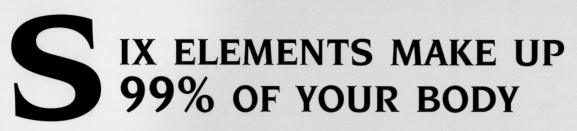

SIX ELEMENTS MAKE UP 99% OF YOUR BODY

Everything around us is made from elements, and so are we! There are just six elements that make up around 99 per cent of your mass and the atoms in your body.

The six elements found in the human body

◁ **Calcium** 1.5% mass
0.25% atoms

Hydrogen ▷
10% mass
63% atoms

◁ **Carbon**
18% mass
9.5% atoms

Phosphorous ▷
1.0% mass
0.20% atoms

◁ **Oxygen**
65% mass
25.6% atoms

Nitrogen ▷
3% mass
1.35% atoms

Calcium is essential for strong teeth and bones.

How do we Know?

More than half of the human body is composed of water (H_2O). Hydrogen and oxygen are the two most common atoms in our body.

About 20 per cent of your body is fat. Too much fat can be bad for you, but some types are necessary to protect your brain cells. Muscles are made from a protein fibre containing hydrogen, carbon, oxygen and nitrogen. Your teeth and bones are made from calcium phosphate.

The science of . . .

For your body to stay in good working order, you need to have a constant supply of the top six elements.

If your body is lacking certain elements, you can take vitamin or mineral supplements.

In addition, your body needs many other elements in small amounts, for example, potassium, sulphur, sodium and magnesium.

We can help our body stay balanced by eating a healthy diet. Many of the elements are found in the foods we eat.

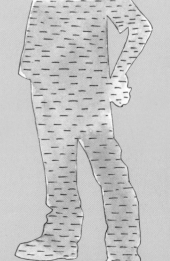

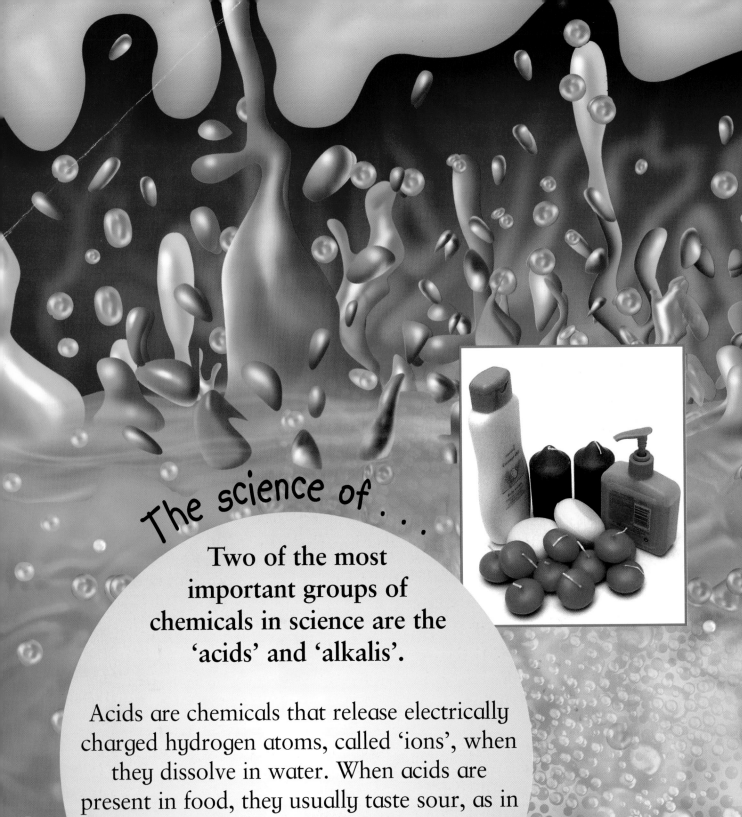

The science of . . .

Two of the most important groups of chemicals in science are the 'acids' and 'alkalis'.

Acids are chemicals that release electrically charged hydrogen atoms, called 'ions', when they dissolve in water. When acids are present in food, they usually taste sour, as in lemon juice or vinegar.

Alkalis are chemically opposite to acids. When the two are added together, one neutralises the other.

How do we Know?

Important acids used in industry are hydrochloric acid, nitric acid and sulphuric acid. These are known as inorganic because they are produced from rocks and ores.

Animals and plants produce inorganic acids, but they also make organic acids. Formic acid, for example, is an irritant in ant bites, bee stings and stinging nettles.

The pH scale measures how acidic or alkaline a substance is, and it ranges from 0 to 14. The red colour of beetroot or blackberries is a natural indicator of pH. In acid solutions the dye from these fruits would turn red. In an alkaline solution it would turn blue. Another way of testing the pH of liquids is to use 'litmus paper'.

Today chemists use electronic pH meters to test the strength of acids and alkalis.

ACID IN YOUR STOMACH CAN 'BURN' ROCKS

We need chemical reactions to help break down the food we eat. Our stomach contains powerful acids which help start this process. Stomach acid is so strong it could 'burn away' rocks like chalk and limestone.

FLAMES ARE STORED SUNLIGHT

Fire is a chemical reaction between oxygen in the air and some sort of fuel. When a flame burns, it releases the chemical energy stored in the fuel that is burning.

How do we know?

All chemical fuels on Earth come from plants. These fuels contain energy.

Plants convert sunlight into energy and this process is called 'photosynthesis'.

For a plant to survive it needs to convert light energy into chemical energy. Photosynthesis combines carbon dioxide and water to form carbohydrates (which plants need to grow) and oxygen (which plants release into the atmosphere).

Plants store sunlight in the form of carbohydrates, and over millions of years this energy is converted into different fossil fuels.

Fossil fuels like coal, gas and oil were formed millions of years ago deep under the Earth's surface.

The science of . . .

All chemical reactions either absorb or release energy.

A flame is a sign that a chemical reaction is giving out a lot of energy. We can see and feel the heat as this reaction takes place.

The colour of a flame gives a good indication of the type of fuel being burned. The blue flame from gas comes from the burning of hydrogen atoms. The orange-yellow flame of a candle comes from the burning of carbon.

The science of...

Satellites and space stations get their power from the Sun.

Electricity is generated when power from the Sun falls directly onto solar panels. However, sometimes the Earth is positioned between the space station and the Sun. Then energy stored in rechargeable batteries is used. These are similar to the one in a mobile phone.

SPACE STATIONS ARE POWERED BY BATTERIES

Where do spacecraft get their power from? Nowadays, satellites and spacecraft, like shuttles and the new international space station, use solar panels. However, they also need batteries to store energy when needed.

How do we know?

The chemical battery was discovered over 200 years ago by Alessandro Volta and Luigi Galvani.

Galvani noticed that dissected frogs' legs would twitch if they were hung from a copper wire. Volta then found if you hung the copper wire from an iron bar, you could produce electricity. This meant it was electricity that made the frogs' legs twitch!

This discovery proved that if two metal wires touch in water, one metal dissolves in a chemical reaction, driving electricity around the wire circuit.

The science of . . .

When we cook
something, the energy we
use is heat.

When we have prepared our food, the
next process is to cook it. No chemical
change occurs until the heat from an oven
causes chemical reactions to take place.

In 1912, a French chemist, Louis-Camille
Maillard, found that sugars and
proteins reacted together
when heated and made
things turn brown.

How do we Know?

Many different chemical reactions can take place in the kitchen:

• Toffee is made by gently heating sugar in an open pan. As the sugar combines with oxygen from the air, the sugar molecules join together and turn brown.

• Sponge (or 'honeycomb') toffee is made by adding vinegar (an acid) and baking soda (a mild alkali) to hot toffee. The acid and the alkali chemically react with one another to release carbon dioxide, making bubbles in the toffee.

Today, a great chef needs to understand as much about the chemistry of cooking as a chemist.

COOKING IS A CHEMICAL REACTION

When we cook food, chemical reactions take place which make it taste different. Next time you take a mouthful, just think what reaction has taken place to make your bread turn brown or your toffee taste different to sugar.

19

How do we Know?

Although air may look like an empty space, it actually contains an incredible number of molecules!

Air is made up of 80 per cent nitrogen and 20 per cent oxygen. We know that one Mole of air (or any gas) contains about 6.02 x 10^{23} particles. That adds up to 602,000 million, million, million molecules!

One Mole of air is estimated to weigh about 30 grams. This means that as you walk around each day, there is a huge weight above your head. This is called 'atmospheric pressure'. We don't feel it because our bodies adjust.

WOWZSAT!

'Mole Day is celebrated from 6:02 a.m. 10/23. The time/ US-style date come from Avogadro's Number (see p21), that is the number of molecules in a Mole.

A CUBIC METRE OF AIR WEIGHS OVER A KILOGRAMME

You are probably surprised to learn that air weighs anything at all! But air contains trillions and trillions of molecules. To enable chemists to talk in such large numbers they invented the 'Mole' – a word that stands for an enormous number!

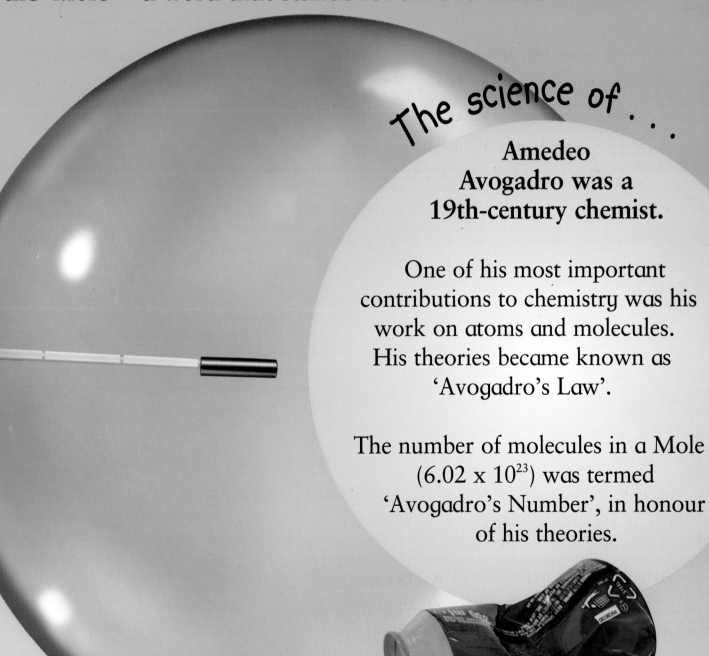

The science of . . .

Amedeo Avogadro was a 19th-century chemist.

One of his most important contributions to chemistry was his work on atoms and molecules. His theories became known as 'Avogadro's Law'.

The number of molecules in a Mole (6.02×10^{23}) was termed 'Avogadro's Number', in honour of his theories.

How do we know?

When a metal rusts, although the surface looks like it is being worn away, the metal atoms are actually combining with oxygen from the air.

Antoine Levoisier was the scientist who first discovered that when chemicals react together, their total mass remains the same. Some substances do lose mass when they combine with oxygen. Coal loses atoms to the air when it burns.

WHEN OBJECTS RUST THEY GET HEAVIER

When metals rust, they lose their shiny appearance and start to disintegrate. This is because atoms on the surface combine with oxygen atoms from the air to produce iron oxide, or 'rust'.

WOWZSAT!

Gold is not like other metals. It does not form an oxide in air and therefore cannot rust. That is one reason why gold is so valuable.

The science of . . .

Most metals will rust if they are exposed to the air for a long time.

One of the most common metals for rusting is iron. Water also encourages this reaction by dissolving oxygen and iron so they react together.

Have you ever seen a statue that has gone green? That is because its copper covering has reacted with sulphur in the air. The green substance is called copper sulphide.

A CUBIC METRE OF SEAWATER CONTAINS OVER 12 KG OF METAL

Take a sip from a glass of tap water. It might taste like nothing but water, but did you know it contains solids? This is what gives water its taste.

The science of...

Anyone who has swum in the sea knows that it is salty.

'Salt' is the common term for any compound of a metal with a non-metal. Seawater has about 36 kg of different salts in every cubic metre of water.

If we evaporate seawater, we are left with a white solid. This is a mixture of different salts.

We get sodium chloride (the salt we eat), from mined underground layers of salt and by drying out seawater.

How do we know?

You will notice that the taste of water changes depending on where you are.

Rainwater does not contain any salts. However, as it seeps through the ground, it dissolves rocks like limestone and chalk. By the time it reaches our taps, it contains many different solids.

Why doesn't the sea get saltier and saltier?

This is because the water is slowly filtered through very hot rocks deep under the floor of the oceans. Here, the dissolved salts form solid rocks.

An average ocean contains about 3.5 per cent solids. The Dead Sea in Israel, however, is landlocked and contains as much as 27 per cent. This means the water is very dense – which makes it easy for people to float!

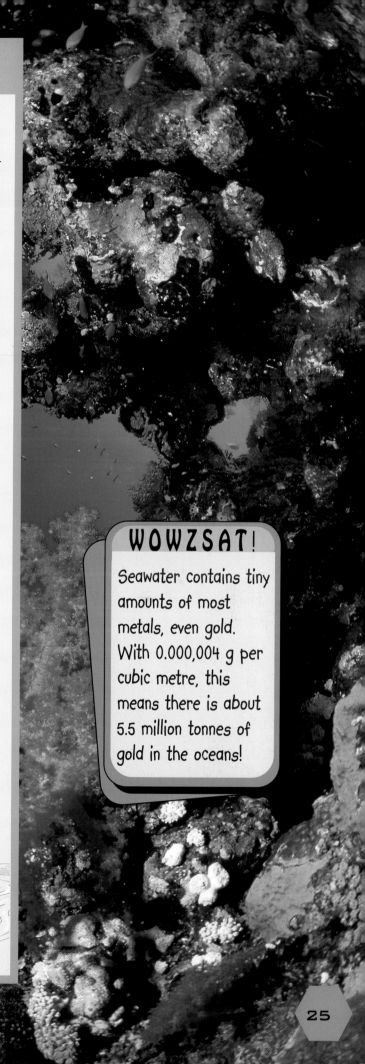

WOWZSAT!

Seawater contains tiny amounts of most metals, even gold. With 0.000,004 g per cubic metre, this means there is about 5.5 million tonnes of gold in the oceans!

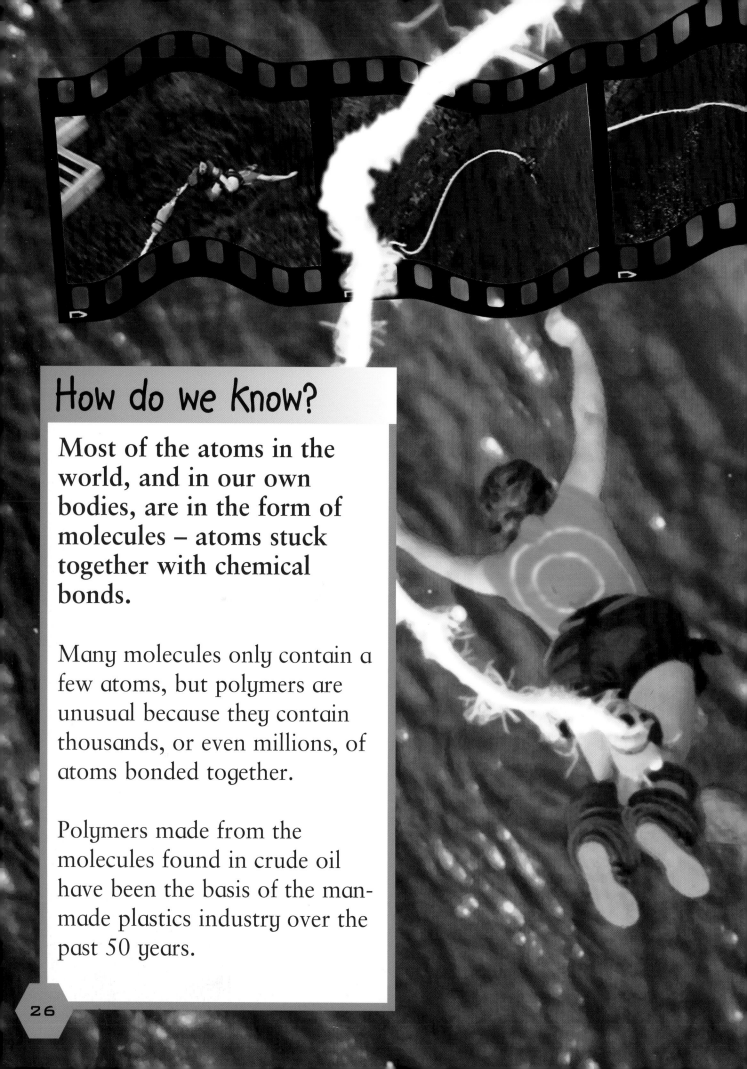

How do we know?

Most of the atoms in the world, and in our own bodies, are in the form of molecules – atoms stuck together with chemical bonds.

Many molecules only contain a few atoms, but polymers are unusual because they contain thousands, or even millions, of atoms bonded together.

Polymers made from the molecules found in crude oil have been the basis of the man-made plastics industry over the past 50 years.

RUBBER CAN STRETCH TO OVER FOUR TIMES ITS NORMAL LENGTH

Have you ever wondered why a rubber (elastic) band is so stretchy? Many 'natural' materials, like wood or oil, are made from long molecules (below) that contain thousands of atoms stuck together. It is how a material is stuck together, that determines how stretchy it is.

The science of . . .

Rubber is a biological molecule made naturally by rubber trees.

A single rubber molecule is a long, thin chain composed of hundreds of thousands of atoms. The molecules in a rubber band are loosely tangled around each other in loops and coils. When you pull a rubber band, the molecules straighten out so that the band becomes longer.

Resin, from pine trees, is a sticky substance because it contains short-chain molecules.

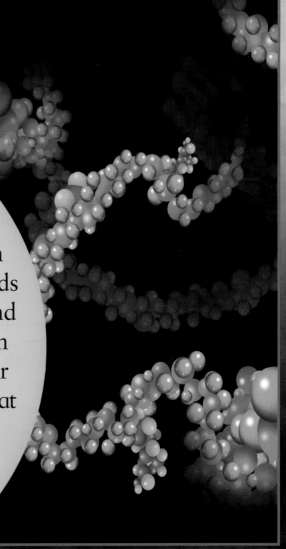

A fire gives out light because it is hot.

As the carbon and hydrogen of the fuel combine with oxygen, the flames and embers are heated by the energy released.

Some animals, such as the firefly (lightning bug) and the glowworm, can produce light without getting hot.

Some fish and jellyfish can also produce light using a process called chemiluminescence.

How do we know?

All chemical reactions absorb and release energy.

Different enzymes are used to control every chemical reaction that takes place in animals and plants. Enzymes are a group of molecules that support other molecules as they react, and can control the speed of the reaction.

Fireflies have a special light organ located under their abdomens. The insects take in oxygen and, inside special cells, combine an enzyme called luciferase with another molecule called luciferin. When luciferin burns in oxygen, it does not lose energy. Instead it produces a light with almost no heat.

ANIMALS CAN MAKE COLD LIGHT FROM CHEMICALS

We are used to seeing hot objects like fire or a light bulb giving out light. Did you know that some plants and animals can glow in the dark without burning themselves?

WOWZSAT!

During World War II, Japanese pilots used to carry dried fireflies. By adding water to the powder, they could produce enough light to read a map at night.

Glossary

Acid – A liquid with a high concentration of hydrogen ions.

Alkali – A liquid with a low concentration of hydrogen ions.

Atom – The smallest piece of an element.

Bond – A link between two atoms.

Compound – A chemical made up of two or more atoms.

Electron – A negatively-charged particle that surrounds the nucleus of an atom.

Element – A substance that contains only one type of atom.

Enzyme – A protein that controls the speed of a reaction.

Ion – An electrically-charged atom or molecule.

Mole – A unit used to describe very large numbers of atoms and molecules.

Molecule – Two or more connected atoms.

Nucleus – The centre of an atom.

Periodic Table – *see below*.

Photosynthesis – A process that plants use to convert sunlight into chemicals.

Polymer – A long chain molecule that is made by combining smaller molecules.

Radioactive – Radioactive substances have a nucleus that spontaneously disintegrates or decays, emitting high-energy particles.

Periodic Table – A diagram (below) that lists all the elements based upon their chemical properties.

	H																	He
	Li	Be											B	C	N	O	F	Ne
	Na	Mg											Al	Si	P	S	Cl	Ar
	K	Ca	Sc	Ti	V	Cr	Mn	Fe	Co	Ni	Cu	Zn	Ga	Ge	As	Se	Br	Kr
	Rb	Sr	Y	Zr	Nb	Mo	Tc	Ru	Rh	Pd	Ag	Cd	In	Sn	Sb	Te	I	Xe
	Cs	Ba	La	Hf	Ta	W	Re	Os	Ir	Pt	Au	Hg	Tl	Pb	Bi	Po	At	Rn
	Fr	Ra	Ac	Rf	Db	Sg	Bh	Hs	Mt	Ds								

1. Non-metals 2. Alkali metals 3. Alkaline earth metals 4. Transition metals
5. Metals 6. Halogens 7. Noble gases 8. Rare earth elements

Ce	Pr	Nd	Pm	Sm	Eu	Gd	Tb	Dy	Ho	Er	Tm	Yb	Lu
Th	Pa	U	Np	Pu	Am	Cm	Bk	Cf	Es	Fm	Md	No	Lr

Biography

Amedeo Avogadro (1776-1856)
An Italian chemist who studied atoms and molecules.

Luigi Galvani (1737-1798)
An Italian anatomist whose early experiments contributed towards the discovery of electricity.

Antoine Lavoisier (1743-1794)
A French scientist who is often regarded as the 'father of chemistry'.

Dimitri Mendeleev (1834-1907)
A Russian chemist who devised the Periodic Table.

Glenn Seaborg (1912-1999)
An American scientist who changed lead into gold.

Alessandro Volta (1745-1827)
An Italian scientist who invented the Voltaic cell – the first electric battery.

KEY DATES

1780 – Luigi Galvani experiments with electrical charges.

1800 – Alessandro Volta designs the first electric battery.

1811 – Amedeo Avogadro studies the amount of atoms in a particular volume of gas.

1869 – Dimitri Mendeleev proposes the 'Periodic Table'.

1912 – Louis-Camille Maillard discovers that sugars and proteins react together when heated, and turn brown.

1980 – Glenn Seaborg successfully turns atoms of lead into atoms of gold, using a nuclear reactor.

Index

Photocredits: l-left, r-right, b-bottom, t-top, c-centre, m-middle. Front cover c, 14-15 – Digital Vision. Front cover bl – Corbis. 1m, 15r, 16b, 18m, 24br – Flick Smith. 2-3, 28-29 – David Godwin/Q2A Creative. 4bl, 24-25 – Stockbyte/Q2A Creative. 4br, 22-23 – Corel. 5t, 8-9 – Flat Earth/Q2A Creative. 5tm, 26-27 – African Extreme. 5m, 18-19 Corbis/ Flick Smith. 5bm, 20-21 – Darren Holloway/Q2A Creative. 6br – World Gold Council www.gold.org. 11tl – Image Library. 12m – Select Pictures. 16-17 – NASA/Flick Smith. 21br, 23bl – www.freeimages.co.uk. 27br – Q2A Creative. 28tr – www.glowcolours.com.